MANAGING 21st CENTURY CLASSROOMS

How do I avoid ineffective classroom management practices?

Jane
BLUESTEIN

ASCD Alexandria, VA USA

ASCD | arias™

Website: www.ascd.org   www.ascdarias.org
E-mail: books@ascd.org

Printed in the United States of America. Cover art © 2014 by ASCD. ASCD publications present a variety of viewpoints. The views expressed or implied in this book should not be interpreted as official positions of the Association.

ASCD LEARN TEACH LEAD® and ASCD ARIAS™ are trademarks owned by ASCD and may not be used without permission. All other referenced trademarks are the property of their respective owners.

PAPERBACK ISBN: 978-1-4166-1885-0   ASCD product #SF114046
Also available as an e-book (see Books in Print for the ISBNs).

Library of Congress Cataloging-in-Publication Data
Bluestein, Jane.
  Managing 21st century classrooms : how do I avoid ineffective classroom management practices? / Jane Bluestein.
      pages cm
  Includes bibliographical references.
  ISBN 978-1-4166-1885-0 (pbk. : alk. paper) 1. Classroom management. I. Title.
  LB3013.B547 2014
  371.102′4--dc23

                                        2013050717

21 20 19   3 4 5 6 7 8 9 10

MANAGING 21st CENTURY CLASSROOMS

How do I avoid ineffective classroom management practices?

Want to earn a free ASCD Arias e-book?
Your opinion counts! Please take 2–3 minutes to give
us your feedback on this publication. All survey
respondents will be entered into a drawing to
win an ASCD Arias e-book.

Please visit
www.ascd.org/ariasfeedback

Thank you!

The Challenge of Classroom Management

You've probably already figured this out: despite the enormous amount of planning and preparation teachers do, instruction is actually the easy part.

See if this sounds familiar: you spend hours designing that perfect lesson. You bring in enrichment activities and related literature, and you're able to make adjustments for kids who need to go back and fill in a few pieces they missed along the way. Your directions are clear, your materials are organized (maybe even color-coded), and you have backup plans in case the lesson runs short. You are enthusiastic and well prepared.

And yet . . .

You're having trouble getting your students to settle down, stop talking, or even get in their seats. One student wants to go to the bathroom while another needs to sharpen a pencil. There's a student making noises, another poking the child in the next seat, and a few others distracted with unrelated tasks or staring off into space. And then there's that seemingly interested child who asks a question that somehow gets you off track, heading in an entirely different direction from the one you had planned.

Let's not forget the students who can't focus because they're hungry, didn't get enough sleep, or are fuming over a nasty encounter they had on the way to your class. There are a few kids who love the topic but need something to do with their hands or their bodies to stay attentive, and some who just can't sit still for one more minute. Add in the students who gave up before they even walked into your class and the ones easily provoked to arguments, defiance, outbursts, or violence, and I suspect that you're not only struggling to accomplish any of the instructional goals you've set, but also going home at the end of the day feeling frustrated, angry, and a bit defeated.

A Big-Picture Issue

Uncooperative student behavior is only one of several reasons why so many teachers are leaving the profession. Of all the reasons mentioned in research surveys and interviews, however, this one consistently appears at the top of the list and is mentioned as a significant source of frustration for many people in the field (Bluestein, 2010).

I believe this happens for a number of reasons. For one, we tend to think of uncooperative or disruptive behavior as something we need to *react* to, and most recommendations we receive, if we actually get any training in this area at all, tend to emphasize a "what-do-I-do-when . . ." approach to classroom management. Unfortunately, the fact that so many of these strategies either do not work or actually make things worse has not seemed to diminish our reliance on them.

We come from a culture that tends to look at situations through an all-or-nothing lens: either *we* are in control or *they* are. We also have traditions that require assigning blame and exacting some type of punishment when infractions occur. Our most familiar classroom management practices reflect a win-lose slant that leaves little room for an approach that would accommodate the teacher's need for authority *as well as* students' need for autonomy within limits (which they likewise need). In this traditional context, it's easy to assume that anything short of an ironhanded, authoritarian attitude toward discipline is flat-out permissive, although this common belief is not remotely true.

Another factor in our difficulty with classroom management is the dissonance between the rapid pace of change in our culture—socially, technologically, and economically, for a start—and the decades-old curriculum, instruction, and management techniques that still form the foundation of our educational systems. For example, consider the rapid shift we have made from the uniformity inherent in an industrial society to the very different needs of one built to deliver information and services. Although assembly-line jobs have all but disappeared from the United States and many other developed countries, the factory-era notion of standardization, especially in curriculum and assessment, remains an intractable cornerstone of how we push kids through school (Bluestein, 1988, 2008, 2010).

Although young people once depended on a handful of adults to give them information on every subject, nowadays an entire world of data and resources is only a click away. Author and educator Sir Ken Robinson suggests that one of the problems with current attempts at school reform around the world is that "they're trying to meet the future by doing what they did in the past. And on the way, they're alienating millions of kids who don't see any purpose in going to school." He also notes that "our children are living in the most intensely stimulating period in the history of the earth. They're being besieged with information . . . and we're penalizing them for getting distracted" from what he refers to as "boring stuff at school" (RSA, 2010). Long for the "good old days" all you want, but there is no going back. It's long past time for our interactive and instructional strategies to catch up to the kids we're teaching—and to the marketplace for which we are ostensibly preparing them.

When we actually do get down to talking about classroom management, our focus tends to be far too narrow. We need to look at this topic from a big-picture perspective. A truly effective approach requires us to pay attention not just to student behavior and power dynamics but also to the pace and content of the curriculum, the social and emotional climate of the classroom, students' belief in their ability to achieve academic success, and the methods of instruction that make sense to the ways individual students learn. *All* of these ingredients affect student behavior, and each one is an important part of an effective approach to classroom management.

7 Common Classroom Management Approaches That Work Against Us

Looking at classroom management practices solely as ways to respond to undesirable behavior ignores the potential of alternative strategies that can *prevent* such behavior. Besides, a reactive, punitive approach doesn't work with those kids we simply cannot scare—kids who are impervious to the worst we can throw at them. Such an approach also compromises the emotional safety of the learning environment and creates a great deal of stress (which, neurologically, gets in the way of learning) for everyone in the room. Keeping problems from occurring in the first place is definitely the preferable option.

Yet we humans are creatures of habit. In the absence of specific positive and proactive strategies for dealing with misbehavior, we tend to fall back on what we have learned or experienced throughout our training, if not our lives. Trying an approach that looks different from what everyone else is doing can put teachers—especially new teachers— at risk for everything from ridicule and social alienation within the school culture to poor evaluations, increased scrutiny, or even transfers or dismissals. So it's understandable that we tend to keep doing the same things over and over again, whether or not they work or even make sense. Fortunately, it's possible to use effective alternatives without getting buy-in or involvement from others. As a bonus, the positive outcomes of these alternatives will make you less vulnerable to others' negative reactions: you make yourself a much smaller target of ridicule or recrimination when your kids are on task, cooperative, and making academic progress.

In the following sections, we'll look at some common misconceptions, examine how they lead to problematic classroom management practices, and explore some more positive and effective options to try instead. Please keep in mind that the positive alternatives work best in a win-win environment—that is, one that recognizes the importance of the relationships we build with our students and eliminates the need for kids to compete for power or fight to maintain their dignity. This dynamic will probably be as unfamiliar to students as it is to most adults, so give it time. When kids know we've got their back and see our efforts to accommodate their needs for structure, belonging, success, and autonomy, acting out starts to look pretty silly and pointless.

Misconception 1: Teachers Must Retain All the Power in the Room

Whether we're talking about children or adults, the need for some degree of power or autonomy is standard issue on all models and comes preinstalled at birth. Even people who always defer to others' choices are making a power play: by putting themselves at the mercy of another's preferences or agendas, they always have someone to blame when things don't go well.

Yet even after acknowledging that all of us—teachers and students alike—have a legitimate need for some degree of control, we have a hard time letting go of the all-or-nothing thinking that says in order for someone to win, someone else has to lose. We fear that if we offer *any* power to students, they'll take it all, and chaos will ensue.

This thinking, and the control-based classroom management behaviors that often follow, tend to backfire on us. Very few of us enjoy losing, and even the best sports are likely to fight back when their safety or dignity is at stake. Thus, the harder we try to control or disempower kids, the harder they will push back, whether by exhibiting overt defiance, becoming passive-aggressive, shutting down, acting out, or even hurting themselves. Although seemingly counterproductive, all of these behaviors give students a sense of control in their lives when they cannot achieve this goal in safer, more productive ways.

Our most familiar rules-and-punishment models are no longer the most effective way to go. (If you're thinking, "Wait! We don't have punishments, we have consequences," read on. If the focus is negative, there really isn't much difference between the two.) Even when this approach seems to work, compliance comes at a cost. Veteran teacher Mark Barnes (2013) wrote, "What I failed to comprehend in my 'I'm-the-meanest-teacher-in-the-school' approach was that I had created a classroom based on control, and I was alienating my students." He admits that while his students "may have, on occasion, acquiesced to my list of demands . . . most of the time their compliance came at the price of learning. After all, what child would embrace education in this kind of militant classroom?" (para. 2).

I have also noticed that many of the traditional power plays teachers use to control or correct behavior have little effect on kids who rely on negative reactions to fulfill their need for attention, provoke adults to outbursts to satisfy their need for power, or simply don't care about their teacher's opinion of them or what punishment they might get. These same powering behaviors, however, can significantly increase the stress level for the rest of the class, especially the cooperative, quiet, or sensitive students. Classroom management behaviors that rely on teacher control and students' fear of punishment trigger the brain's survival instincts and suppress the brain functions students need for learning, cognitive processing, and retention (Bluestein, 2001).

Try This Instead: Establishing Win-Win Authority

Although it's easy to agree that students need a sense of structure or limits, we often struggle with the idea that they also need a certain level of power or autonomy. The better you can accommodate both sets of needs for the students in your classroom, the better you'll be able to maintain your authority without needing to control or disempower anyone else. The following tips are a good place to start.

- **Clarify your goals and intentions.** Teachers who aim to inspire student growth and cooperation will naturally exhibit very different behaviors and language from those of teachers who are simply looking for control. Be sure your behavior matches your intentions.

- **Recognize the difference between controlling and being in charge.** Letting students have some autonomy in your classroom (within limits you determine) does not diminish your authority. The best alternative to trying to control students is teaching them to control *themselves*. Controlling kids deprives them of opportunities to learn and practice the important skill of self-management.

- **Pay attention to your words, tone, and body language.** Notice any tendency toward negativity, criticism, contempt, impatience, or threats. This is the classroom management model many of us know best, but behaviors that hint at possible retribution for lack of compliance inhibit learning. Take the pulse of your classroom climate, looking for any patterns in your behavior that might increase the stress level.

- **Aim for prevention, heading off conflicts and power struggles before they occur.** Find ways to let kids "win" within limits that won't make you (or anyone else) lose. The easiest strategies are those that allow students some input in situations that affect them. Not everything is negotiable, of course, but you can certainly give students choices about which activity to do first or which 10 problems to complete from a list of 15. Once they have built up some decision-making muscle, give them even more autonomy—for example, have them design their own projects within certain criteria you determine.

- **Be the one to keep a cool head if a confrontation occurs.** You may be able to defuse a potential outburst simply by agreeing with a frustrated student or redirecting the energy in the confrontation: "I know you wish you didn't have to do this assignment" or "You know, I think we could all use a two-minute break right now."

Misconception 2: Classroom Rules Ensure Good Behavior

Rules are such a sacred cow in education that we rarely bother to question their existence, much less their effectiveness. I suspect that at some point early in all our careers, teachers are encouraged to make classroom rules and post the list on the wall. Although this is a common and familiar practice—I don't think I've ever seen instructions for the first day of school that did not include "go over the rules"—they aren't especially useful in terms of classroom management. They rarely vary from one classroom to the next, tend to be expressed negatively (except when phrased as generic platitudes like "Respect one another"), and do not teach students self-management. Usually rooted in teacher or organizational power, they create an illusion of authority for the adults (something to point to when kids misbehave) and often carry a subtle or explicit threat of reprisal if they are not followed. In general, a focus on rules distracts us from building community and positive outcomes for cooperation, both of which trump a list of rules as far as effective classroom management goes.

Many schools develop a code of conduct and require that rules be posted in each classroom. This is understandable and, from a liability aspect, perfectly reasonable. Aside from the legal implications, however, I think we just do this because we have always done it. The unsettling upshot is reflected in the number of teachers who come to the profession believing that all they need to inspire good behavior is a comprehensive set of rules and are subsequently surprised and dismayed when rules alone don't work.

There is a great deal of mythology around the power of rules, including the implication that simply having rules will inspire students' commitment to them, especially if they're right up on the wall where everyone can see them. If awareness of rules were an effective strategy, however, we could reasonably expect that there would never be any murders, thefts, illegal drug use, or even speeding violations. Yet despite the abundance of well-known rules and punishments for these offenses, such transgressions occur on a daily basis.

When you walk into a classroom where kids are busy and engaged, it is unlikely that their cooperation was motivated by rules. And I can almost guarantee that when students are disruptive, off task, or out of control, it's not because there aren't *enough* rules. In fact, I have noticed that the schools with the longest lists of rules also tend to have the greatest number of behavior problems (Bluestein, 2010).

We have an unfortunate inclination to add more rules any time a new misbehavior occurs, ultimately creating codes of conduct that, at times, border on the absurd. One of my favorite complaints from a high school student was about an injunction against bringing ninja stars to school (Bluestein & Katz, 2005). Is it any wonder we have a hard time getting kids to follow rules, or even respect our authority?

If you are required to post a list of rules, by all means, do so. Be assured, however, that your kids are unlikely to check the list before they misbehave or even notice it after two or three days. And although it may still be a popular practice to have students make their own rules, in my experience I found this approach to be a waste of time that generated no more student commitment than my own lists of rules did. Feel free to skip this one.

Try This Instead: Boundaries with Positive Outcomes

Clearly, students need structure, limits, criteria, and guidelines for everything from engaging in specific activities and using equipment to moving around the classroom and interacting with the teacher and their peers. The way this information is shared sounds different from the way most rules or commands are presented, however. These communications give students the information they need to be successful in each specific endeavor. Positively stated boundaries or contingencies avoid relying on students' fear of punishment and instead emphasize conditions and positive outcomes for cooperation. The following tips will help you encourage constructive behavior without handing down draconian decrees.

- **Keep it simple and positive.** In my own practice, I found that the fewer rules I tried to create and enforce, the more smoothly my classroom operated. My students could pretty much do whatever they wanted as long as their behavior didn't interfere with teaching or learning. Even my younger students quickly figured out just how comprehensive and restrictive that "rule" was. Of course, I needed to delineate specific boundaries and conditions for certain activities or the use of certain equipment, but those fit under the heading of directions rather than actual rules. Focusing on the desirable outcomes they could earn was far more effective than any rules I ever attempted to use.
- **Watch out for all-or-nothing thinking that equates deemphasizing rules with letting kids do whatever they want.** Just as students need a sense of power or control, they need limits, too. To provide the structure they need, give explicit instructions, phrased clearly and positively as boundaries with built-in limits that offer students specific ways of getting something they want: "You can work together as long as it doesn't

create a problem for anyone else," or "You can take another library book home as soon as you return the one you have checked out." Avoid making kids wrong, moralizing, criticizing, or framing contingencies as threats, which emphasize the negative outcomes of failing to do what you've asked rather than the positive outcomes of fulfilling the requirements for the task.

- **Be responsive rather than punitive.** The greatest challenge in making this shift involves letting go of the notion that misbehavior requires some negative retribution. If an infraction occurs, resist the urge to point to the rules or pull out the code-of-conduct booklet to prove you have the right to object. Withhold or withdraw the privilege, ask students to find other seats, or stop reading the story until behavior improves: "Let's try again tomorrow." In some instances, a quiet reminder that "we don't say [or do] that here" will get kids back on track.

Misconception 3: I Shouldn't Have to Motivate My Students

Early in my career, I bought into the notion that intrinsic motivation was preferable to extrinsic motivation. After all, who wouldn't love working with kids who wake up thankful for another opportunity to write essays or do fractions? I had been told that connecting positive student behavior to positive outcomes is bribery, and that this is a bad thing. It took me a while to start wondering why we don't recognize threats of failure, detention, or negative reports to parents as bribes, too; the only difference is that these "bribes" require kids to make the preferred choice out of fear rather than as a way to access a positive outcome that's meaningful and desirable to them.

Over the years, I have concluded that there is no such thing as unmotivated behavior—because all behavior is motivated by *something*—and that every choice satisfies some internal need. Fear of a teacher's reaction, whether it comes in the form of punishment, academic failure, or emotional abandonment (e.g., disapproval, isolation, or rejection), is just as "intrinsic" as love of the subject area or excitement about a specific activity. I also believe that it is just as reasonable (and just as internally driven) for kids to do assignments they don't especially love because they want credit for the assignment or want to get it out of the way to go on to a more desirable activity.

I'm sure we have all met (or had) teachers who just wanted to come in and talk about their topic or hand out assignments and not be bothered with little details like making the work meaningful or worthwhile to students. I have heard many a teacher say things like, "I shouldn't have to motivate my students." Perhaps this is because motivation can require a good bit of work, connecting with kids to discover what drives them and how they learn best. More likely, though, this mind-set is based in an entrenched belief that promising any meaningful, positive outcome instead of simply expecting each student to show up with an automatic, innate love of learning reflects poorly on our skills as professionals. That's a misconception long overdue for letting go.

Try This Instead: Use Positive Motivators to Build Commitment and Cooperation

Connecting a desirable outcome to a less desirable task is a legitimate and necessary part of the job of teaching. Accepting the fact that *all* behavior is motivated by some need-fulfilling outcome can help us get over the resentment and annoyance we might feel when our kids don't have the same passion and appreciation for the subject matter or a well-designed lesson that we do. Accepting this reality can also relieve some of the guilt and inadequacy we are taught to feel when we need to get creative to engage students' participation and commitment to a task. The following tips will help you rethink motivation in your classroom.

- **Reexamine the belief system that equates motivation with bad teaching.** We might want to start by thinking about what motivates us to do the work *we* do. I'm certain that most of us would cite a genuine desire to make a difference, our love and concern for our students, and that incredible rush we get when we see the light go on in a child's eyes. But let's not discount the fact that many of us also choose teaching because of the schedule—evening, weekend, and summer work duties notwithstanding—and the salary. I've met very few individuals who would tolerate the challenges of the profession, regardless of the emotional satisfaction they experience, without getting a paycheck and benefits. Do the value and importance of these external motivators negate our commitment to the profession? We can let go of this double standard when we recognize that kids need meaningful motivators, too.

- **Increase the odds that students will succeed at the tasks they are assigned.** It's very hard to love learning when success always seems to be out of reach. Students who believe they're going to fail no matter what have little stake in engaging and cooperating. On the other hand, if you support students in their learning and give them manageable assignments, they are much more likely to willingly engage in tasks.

Success and academic progress can be tremendously motivating. Even in classrooms where content and daily activities are assigned at the district level, I have seen teachers pull aside students to fill in learning gaps and catch them up. When we fail to connect our instruction to students' current ability, kids who lack skills or knowledge they need to succeed fall further and further behind. On the other hand, starting a lesson with something students are able to do can have a powerful effect: I've seen kids who, after experiencing some level of success for the first time, made surprising leaps far beyond where they had started. Let's remember that we teach *students;* the content is *always* secondary. Being able to understand a concept or successfully complete an assignment opens the door to the possibility of actually finding intrinsic joy in the content, or even in being in school.

- **Start thinking of consequences as the positive outcome of cooperation.** I realize that the word *consequence* is almost always used interchangeably with the word *punishment*. Even when we try to differentiate the two terms, we still end up focusing on negative outcomes for negative behaviors. So this is an important shift, and it is quite doable, although it will require a willingness to drop our reliance on threats and negative reactions, including using anger, disappointment, or conditional approval to generate the behaviors we want.

  Even making a simple change from a threat ("If you don't do this, you *can't* . . .") to a promise ("As soon as you do this, you *can* . . .") transforms the energy and power dynamic in the interaction and increases the likelihood of cooperation, especially if the positive outcome is meaningful to students. Offer a variety of positive consequences to accommodate a range of student interests and learning styles.

- **Be clear about which positive outcomes are available and how students can attain them.** Telling a class, "If you're good, we might have a surprise on Friday" fails on several counts. First, students are likely to misunderstand what being "good" means because the teacher failed to explain the specific behaviors required. Second, "a surprise" could be anything from pizza and a movie to a pop quiz. Why would students work for something they don't care about or want? Finally, the word *might* implies that a surprise might *not* be forthcoming, regardless of the class's behavior. If students can't be sure of a positive outcome, why would they bother trying to earn it?

It is also important to provide positive outcomes in a timely manner, ensuring that the privilege is not delayed to the point of uselessness. Working for a diploma and college acceptance may be appropriate for a high-achieving, goal-oriented high school senior, but Friday may be too far away for a struggling 5th grader who needs encouragement, a different activity, or a short break right now.

• **Accept the choices we make.** I have a plea: let's stop judging ourselves and others for making the choices we make to get kids on board, behaviorally and academically, by satisfying what seems to be the most important need at that moment. I have had kids do assignments because they loved the task and others who stayed caught up because doing so allowed them to work in an enrichment center later or help out in another class. The fact that they were on task, making progress, and not obstructing others' learning was the part that mattered, far more than how they got there.

Misconception 4: Conditional Praise Is Necessary and Effective

Teachers have received a fair amount of encouragement to use praise as a classroom management tool. All learners need positive reinforcement and feedback, of course. Although recognizing effort, persistence, or a job well done is legitimate and valuable, there are a number of ways to get this one wrong, with potentially harmful results.

One of the most common problems occurs when a teacher publicly praises one student in order to encourage others to act in a similar way. This usually occurs in classrooms with younger students, where the teacher will say, for example, "I like the way Lisa is sitting" in an effort to get Bart to sit the same way.

I immediately see two problems here. First, the praise communicates conditional acceptance: Lisa is valued because she is doing what Teacher wants. Second, it is quite likely that Bart just won't care. In addition, if Lisa is embarrassed by being held up as an example for the class or values her peers' approval more than the teacher's, this statement may backfire and result in a display of far less desirable behavior from Lisa. Recognition and reinforcement are meant to be used *after* a behavior occurs, not as a way to elicit desirable behaviors.

In addition to connecting a student's behavior to the teacher's pleasure or happiness, praise is often vague and focused on a singular aspect of a child's skills, capabilities, or personality. It seems fairly innocuous to tell kids that they're smart or creative or athletic, but something interesting happens when we emphasize one of these characteristics over behaviors they have more control over—say, the time and effort they devoted to a project.

Researcher Carol Dweck (2013) found that the quality of the feedback we give to students affects not only their self-concept but also their confidence and willingness to challenge themselves with more difficult tasks. She discovered that when children who were praised for their intelligence ("You must be really smart") were given a choice between staying at the level at which they received praise or going on to a more difficult activity, they tended to choose easier tasks where they could continue to be successful and maintain the appearance of being smart. When they run into trouble, these students are apt to say, "Oh, I'm not very good at that." They are reluctant to put themselves in a position in which they might fail or be judged as "not smart."

On the other hand, children who were recognized for their effort ("You must have tried really hard") were far more willing to attempt more challenging tasks, and they perceived obstacles and failure as signs that they just needed to work a bit more or take a different approach. "Children praised for effort generally want those hard [tasks] that they can learn from," Dweck (2013) observes.

Try This Instead: Recognition and Feedback Without Labels

There is a danger in using *any* kind of label with kids, if for no other reason than it reduces complex human beings to a single, simplistic dimension of their identity, based on a perception that may or may not be accurate. Sure, our brains are wired to categorize what we encounter to make sense of the world around us, and if we're talking about food groups or music genres, that's just fine and dandy. But labeling or categorizing students—even positively—not only influences other adults who deal with those children but also limits kids' perceptions of who they are and what they are capable of achieving. The following tips will help you avoid these pitfalls in your class.

- **Become aware of how you use labels.** Notice how often you refer to students, both in and out of earshot, with one-word or one-dimensional labels. Listen to how you ask for behaviors from your students. Do you tend to talk about how much you like the behavior of a given student or group to elicit similar conduct from the others? How likely are you to focus on effort (as opposed to characteristics such as intelligence) in your feedback? Watch out for labels, even positive ones. Whether you're providing information to a parent or colleague or giving feedback to the kids themselves, focus on specific examples of performance and effort instead.
- **Know your intentions and use appropriate strategies.** It is important to ascertain what your goal

is and choose an approach accordingly. For example, if your intention is to elicit a behavior you have not seen yet, you need to use a different approach from the one you use to reinforce existing desirable behavior. The first goal requires a motivational strategy, such as providing a positive outcome for the desired behavior: "As long as your report is finished by the final bell on Thursday, you can work in the media center on Friday." (Note: Be specific about what "finished" means.)

However, if you want to reinforce the student's behavior when he or she turns in the report, switch to a recognition statement: "Hey, you got your report in on time. You have earned your hour in the media center." Reinforcement happens *after* the desirable behavior has occurred. The goal is to describe the positive behavior (rather than praising it) and then connect the behavior to the positive outcome. This strategy also helps build responsibility by helping students see the connection between their choices and the privilege they earn as a result.

- **Feel free to show your appreciation.** Despite all the caveats connected to praise and labels, a genuine expression of appreciation is not likely to be a problem. Simple recognition ("Wow! You really put a lot of time into this" or "You know, your character descriptions were really detailed") that emphasizes students' efforts and actions rather than how their behavior pleases you is a great way to build morale and positive relationships.

There will be times when your kids delight and amaze you, and there is no reason to hide your pleasure or enjoyment. Kids of all ages learn better in an environment where they feel valued by the teacher. In fact, according to retired superintendent Robert Reasoner, a student's perception that "my teacher cares about me" is the single most important factor in his or her potential school success, regardless of age, gender, socioeconomic status, quality of home life, or actual academic ability (Bluestein, 2001). This crosses the line only when we use conditional teacher approval as a management tool, suggesting that our feelings about our students depend on how they act or the quality of their work.

- **Use activities, not prizes, to encourage positive behavior.** Giving out stickers or tokens as rewards for good behavior can create more problems than it solves. For one thing, the tokens are superficial and tend to be distributed in a fairly arbitrary manner, leaving some cooperative or quiet kids overlooked. Second, keeping track of the tokens, dealing with lost tokens, and making time to trade in tokens is a time-consuming pain in the neck. (I know. I tried.) Using activities as positive reinforcement—letting students do something meaningful and fun, which can include instructional activities or helping others—is far more effective in terms of building commitment, cooperation, and responsibility.

Misconception 5: Giving Warnings and Asking for Excuses Are Acceptable Strategies

As we know, structure and limits provide a sense of safety and predictability for our students; they also allow for students' needs for autonomy to be expressed without creating problems for others. But structure is only as effective as our willingness to follow through on the conditions and limits we use to create it. I suspect that this is what our instructors meant, back in our teacher preparation classes, when they referred to the need for "consistency": allowing what we offer *only* under the conditions we offer it.

I'm sure that most people would agree with the merit of this advice, but unfortunately, we have developed a number of bad habits that consistently get in our way, undermining our authority and our students' respect for the limits we set. If you see yourself in any of the following examples, you are in good company: many of these patterns have become institutionalized traditions that are well ingrained in our culture and our profession.

For example, if I assign a homework task and set a deadline that gives my students a reasonable amount of time to complete it, it is entirely reasonable to give credit only to those who turn in the work. Yet we all know that even the best intentions of our most committed students can be waylaid or interrupted by other priorities, and frankly, some of our kids have so much going on in their lives that it's a near miracle they stay caught up in school at all. So it seems reasonable, when they don't have the work done, to ask why. But let's look at the damage that simple question can do.

When we ask for excuses, we put ourselves in the position of judging the worthiness of those excuses. Our judgment will likely be influenced by our feelings about this particular student, the student's history of turning in work on time, and our mood at that moment. At the same time, we imply that our acceptance of the excuse depends on the student's ability to be creative and at least a little pathetic.

Asking for excuses or explanations when students have misbehaved, broken an agreement, or failed to complete an assignment interferes with our goal of building responsibility by suggesting that students can talk their way out of the requirements we set. This is not only time-consuming but also emotionally exhausting, as well as a really good way of encouraging kids not to take our limits seriously.

Further, there is really no equitable way to judge excuses and decide who gets a pass and who doesn't. It is all too easy for some students to get away with an extension while others don't simply because of your feelings about the students, because you are not impressed with what might be a perfectly legitimate reason, or simply because you aren't feeling especially generous that day. In addition, a good bit of research (Bluestein, 2001) and anecdotal evidence show that teachers are more likely to cut certain students more slack than others when it comes to homework, attendance, tardiness, and other discipline-related matters. Students who come from wealthier families, who dress well, or who are academically or athletically gifted are more likely to enjoy leniency not accorded to students who do not fall into these groups.

Another way we sabotage our authority is by reacting to infractions with warnings instead of following through on the conditions we set. For example, let's say I tell a group of students that they are allowed to work together as long as their interactions don't interfere with the work I'm doing with another group. If their behavior does get disruptive, the effective response would be to withdraw the privilege immediately. But how much easier would it be just to turn around in my seat and tell them to quiet down or ask, "What did I say?"

Lack of follow-through is a persistent problem in our field. Years ago, it became popular to write the name of a misbehaving student on the board, adding check marks for subsequent offenses until, after a certain number of checks, the student was sent to the office. This widely used strategy had the unfortunate side effect of actually reinforcing the misbehavior of students who were acting out for attention; most teachers who tried this technique found that they were writing the same names on the board all year long. I have also heard stories of kids competing to see who could get their name up there first (or who could get the most checks), as well as reports from "good" kids who found it difficult to learn with the distractions and stress this approach created for *them*.

Over the years, this model has been replaced with a variety of other warning systems, including using cues such as colored cards and stoplights, which all communicate the same thing to our students: "You don't have to listen, cooperate, or take me seriously *until. . ."*

Try This Instead: Improving Follow-Through

The best way to improve follow-through (and thus maintain respect and authority) is to *only* allow positive outcomes when they are earned and withdraw them when the conditions are violated. When we can shift our classroom management mind-set from seeking out bigger and better punishments to offering more enticing privileges, we can increase the number of positive consequences we offer, which gives students lots of incentives for cooperating with our policies, requirements, and requests. As a side benefit, when these privileges can accommodate neurological and learning preferences—for example, allowing students to move around or listen to music during seatwork—we end up improving not only students' behavior but also their learning. The following tips will help you increase follow-through in your policies and practices.

- **Anticipate what you will need to make your policies work.** Taking time to figure out the criteria you will require for different activities will enable you to communicate them clearly when it comes time to explain what you're asking or allowing students to do. Providing good directions with clear boundaries can eliminate the temptation to give warnings or ask for excuses.

- **Pay attention to timing.** Follow-through is about helping students earn and enjoy privileges, credit, or accommodations for their preferences. As soon as one of the conditions is breached, it is important to revoke the privilege in a calm, nonpunitive manner, as a simple, factual outcome of the breach: "This isn't working," "Please find other places to work," or "We can try this again tomorrow." There is no reason to make them wrong or point out the errors of their ways when they blow it. The lack of access to the privilege is far more powerful than are words describing what they did wrong.
- **Build parent support by communicating your policies early on.** Parents are far more likely to respect your requirements when they know what they are, when they see a built-in safety net (which saves them the inconvenience of needing to write excuse notes or go to bat for their child), and when they have a sense that you follow through consistently.
- **Watch your tendency to over-explain.** We are especially likely to over-talk our reasons for following through when we lack confidence in our ability to actually *do* it, particularly if we are nervous about the reaction of our students (or their parents). Such explanations can turn into lectures, criticisms, or pleas to students to accept our decision to pull the plug on a certain privilege. This undermines our authority and is usually a waste of breath: kids can tune out adults

the second we open our mouths. They learn far more from our actions than our words.

- **Build some flexibility into your policy *before* a problem occurs.** Students do have other things going on in their lives, and everyone has a bad night from time to time, so it makes sense to build some leeway into our policies—as long as we do it ahead of time. This works especially well for homework or longer-term projects. For example, I have known teachers who gave their students a homework pass they could use to delay an assignment once or twice a semester. One teacher required students to turn in 37 out of 40 assignments on time each semester for full credit, while another allowed students who didn't finish an assignment in class to turn in the work by the last bell of the school day.

- **Create a positive climate and build strong relationships.** Class climate and relationships play a big part in students' willingness to earn—or temporarily lose—a privilege. You reduce the likelihood of an argument when kids see you working to accommodate their needs and preferences, when their dignity and emotional safety are not at stake, and when they figure out that you're not a pushover because you stick to your policy.

Misconception 6: Administrators and Parents Can Take Care of Discipline

There was a time when being sent to the principal carried a certain degree of terror and social stigma. Not so much today. As administrative roles have shifted toward instructional leadership, many of the principals I have met frankly resent being used to handle misbehavior that occurs in the classroom, especially requests to punish students for infractions like talking out of turn, chewing gum, or coming to class unprepared. Teachers are even more likely to be seen in a negative light when they send students to the office for acting out because of something the teacher said or did that the student experienced as hostile, humiliating, or threatening.

Seeking advice, feedback, or ideas from your principal, school counselor, and other support personnel or keeping them apprised of changes in a student's performance or behavior is legitimate and professional. Counting on them to take an annoying student off your hands or to punish students for something they did not witness is not. Regardless of the degree of justification you may feel, depending on another professional to deal with your discipline problems will be seen as an indication that you can't handle your kids—not only by your administrators and colleagues but also by parents and the students themselves.

Speaking of parents, regular feedback about their children's school experiences is almost always valued—especially when it includes positive notes, progress updates, and work samples—but I have met very few who appreciate expectations that they will solve teachers' problems for them, and calling a parent to complain about a student's behavior will likely be perceived as exactly that. Plus, even if parents do try to take care of the problem, there is no guarantee that their responses will be what you want or expect.

Certainly, parents' reactions will be influenced by the type of contact you have had with them before, so if you have already established a positive relationship, updating them about changes or concerns may not be a problem. However, the teachers who most often describe parents' reactions as anything from indifferent to hostile tend to be the ones who get in touch only when there is a problem. Further, parents who see their child's misbehavior or failure as a reflection of their parenting skills—and many will—may not only become defensive with you but also take out their embarrassment or annoyance on their children. Tempting as this may seem at times, this really is not the kind of support you want.

Try This Instead: Building a Support System

If you have noticed the topic of relationships cropping up repeatedly throughout this publication, know that it is intentional. Not only do positive, mutually respectful relationships minimize discipline problems and increase student learning and engagement, but they also increase support and cooperation from the adults in your professional life.

Most of the tips in this section come back to building connections with parents, students, and colleagues as a means of gaining vital support, even as you accept that the buck stops with you.

- **Assume ultimate responsibility for your students' behavior.** Just as you encourage personal responsibility and accountability in your students, it's important to assume the role of responsible adult in your own classroom. Shifting your focus away from punishments (negative consequences) and instead creating a positive climate that offers privileges contingent on cooperative and on-task behavior will help reduce many of the problems teachers commonly encounter. Look to school administrators, support staff, and parents as resources for feedback and ideas rather than holding them responsible for solving your management problems.

- **Build relationships with parents.** There are a number of ways to keep parents in the loop without insisting that they correct their child's behavior, much less help you maintain order in your classroom. Initiate some form of positive contact with parents early in the year, before any problems arise—if possible, before you've even met your students. Keep the focus on how much you enjoy (or anticipate enjoying) working with their child and what you hope to accomplish during the first few weeks rather than clobbering them with pages of rules and policies. Share any intentions you can reasonably expect to keep up with, such as providing a list of assignments or work samples on your class or school website throughout the year or sending out a monthly newsletter.

In addition, sending folders home each week with completed work—and, better yet, a short checklist or bit of feedback—is never a bad idea. One of the most significant boosts I experienced in my relationships with parents came when I started sending out weekly progress reports for my most challenging classes. It rarely took me more than 15 minutes at the end of each week to complete these "good notes," which focused on progress and positive behavior. An amazing percentage of these notes found their way home, even among my older students, who I initially assumed would be indifferent to these communications. Occasional calls or e-mails home when a child has had a big breakthrough, made significant improvement in work or behavior, or even just had a good day can build a strong positive alliance with parents. Do be sure to keep track of whose parents you call so that all of your students eventually get a positive personal message. This is one practice that can benefit every one of your students—and you!

In the event that you do need to contact a parent about a problem, your previous efforts to maintain regular positive contact will likely have created a connection that makes it easier to do so. Focus discussions on specific behavior or performance issues and avoid comments or judgments about personality.

Parents of students who are struggling academically, behaviorally, or socially deserve to hear about it long before the problem interferes with their children's academic success, advancement, or graduation.

Check and recheck all correspondence for spelling and grammatical errors. If you have any doubt at all, get another pair of eyes to check for clarity and tone as well. Send copies to the office to keep on record, and maintain a paper trail (whether physical or electronic) of all contact with parents—not just paper or e-mail exchanges, but also the dates and content of phone conversations and face-to-face meetings. You may never use these materials, but it is a sure bet you will regret not having them if you ever need them.

- **Keep files on your students.** In a profession in which demands for paperwork and "administrivia" seem to increase annually, it may seem unreasonable to recommend keeping student files, but I'm going to anyway. These files can include work samples, pre-test and post-test results, behavior checklists, and anecdotal notes about any patterns you see in students' behavior or learning styles. If you ever need to support or explain decisions to recommend special help or placement, teach in a certain way, accommodate individual learning needs, repeat a lesson, or push a student beyond immediate curricular mandates, this documentation will be the best friend you ever had.
- **Get collegial support.** Despite the importance of assuming responsibility for your students' behavior,

all teachers need support, and if you have a good relationship with your administrators and can depend on them to observe you and give you good, honest feedback, so much the better. If this seems out of reach—whether because your administrators have agendas that differ significantly from your goals and intentions or because you suspect that they may use any difficulties you encounter as an excuse to attack rather than help you—find a colleague you can trust. The point of this collaboration is to open yourself to different perspectives, solutions you may not have previously considered, and opportunities for personal and professional growth.

Misconception 7: Kids Will Not Learn Without Negative Consequences

Before beginning their practice, many doctors swear the Hippocratic Oath, promising to do their best by the patients entrusted to their care. I have often wondered if we in the teaching profession need a similar tradition, not only to protect our charges but also to remind us of the numerous practices that would violate such a commitment. The closest version we have can be found in the National Education

Association's (1975) Code of Ethics, which defines a commitment to students that would prohibit many of the practices people experience, witness, and use in schools every day.

I have walked down the halls of schools hearing little but loud commands and criticisms behind each door I passed. If *I* was unnerved by this experience, what must it have been like for the kids who were stuck in those rooms all day? Try to imagine how much learning could possibly take place in such an environment. Add the threat of physical retribution—sadly, a reality in the U.S. states that still have legislation permitting the long-outdated practice of corporal punishment—and we increase the risk of even more severe negative outcomes (Bluestein, 2001).

Many adults believe that children cannot learn without being on the receiving end of some repercussion intended to create discomfort, embarrassment, or pain. This is a grave misconception. When we perceive threat, our primary brain functions retreat to the survival centers of the midbrain. A teacher's anger or contempt, or even impatience or disappointment, can trigger a fight, flight, or freeze response that impedes learning by blocking access to more rational, cognitive parts of the brain. Whether targets or witnesses, most individuals exposed to this energy will either shut down or fight back, with a no-win outcome likely for all concerned (Bluestein, 2001). Kids who don't feel safe, valued, or liked by their teachers have little stake in making classroom management particularly easy for them.

A few practices are so entrenched in our profession that we rarely bother to question their effectiveness. One of these involves labeling the misbehavior and sounds something like this: "That's unacceptable" or "You're being rude." I have heard teachers argue how important it is to let kids know what they're doing wrong without realizing that these comments give students absolutely no information about what more desirable behavior looks like. Making kids wrong comes from a need for satisfaction and revenge; it rarely provides much in the way of actual instruction or guidance.

Another popular strategy that just won't seem to go away is the use of I-messages (or I-statements), formulaic comments that connect teachers' feelings to students' behavior. In other words, they are pleas for students to change their behavior so that *we* will feel better. There are several obvious problems with this tactic, not least of which is the very real possibility that students may not care that we "feel sad and frustrated" when they forget their library book, won't stop talking, or disrupt a lesson. In fact, if students' intentions are to upset us (there is a great deal of power in provoking an emotional reaction from someone else), an attempt to make them responsible for our emotional well-being will only reinforce the behavior we want to stop.

Likewise harmful is imposing academic penalties on students for misbehavior. Punishing students by assigning extra work will likely achieve nothing, other than increasing their disconnectedness and dislike for school. And although I certainly agree that students should be required to complete the work we assign to receive credit, allowing a student's behavior to influence his or her grades, eligibility, placement, promotion, or graduation is petty and unprofessional.

Although some codes of conduct are written in ways to give teachers legitimate reasons to suspend or expel students, let's keep in mind that the potential for gaining academic knowledge as well as learning self-management, respect for others, and basic citizenship skills is more likely to occur in a positive classroom environment than out on the street. Again, a focus on prevention is far more effective than these reactive traditions.

Try This Instead: Creating a Safe Environment

Behaviors such as yelling and shaming interfere with learning, increase stress for teachers, and, in some instances, undermine the ethics and ideals of the profession itself. Most of these patterns are familiar from our own upbringing and built into our cultural reality, if not our institutions. Nonetheless, each instance of hurtful behavior increases the potential for additional conflict and can severely impair the quality of school climate both for the troublemakers and for the rest of the students in the class. The alternative to most of these behaviors is simply to stop doing them. If that seems easier said than done, the following tips should help you begin the process of replacing commonly accepted harmful practices with new, more positive approaches.

- **Be aware of your behavior.** Pay attention to your words, your tone, the volume of your voice, your body language, and your proximity to students you address. It might help you to record a day in the classroom in audio or video format and listen or watch for instances of hurtful, shaming behaviors, including expressions of contempt or even disappointment. Ask yourself if such expressions would be OK if the roles were reversed—if your students addressed you in the same way you speak to them. Respect is a two-way street, so let's model the behaviors we would like to inspire.

- **Put off grading until you're in a positive state of mind.** Grading papers when you're in a bad mood is generally not a good idea. If you're angry at a student (or a student's parent), your feelings could easily influence your assessment. Hold off on evaluating assignments until you can do so objectively. If you're feeling stressed, angry, or even just tired, consider taking a break so your impression of your students' work will not be affected by your mood.

- **Avoid assigning more work as a punishment for misbehavior.** Often, misbehavior occurs because students' needs are not being met. Focus on prevention by building community and belonging, offering choices that grant students freedom within limits, assigning challenging work that students can do successfully, and teaching in whatever ways make sense to different students' bodies, brains, and learning styles.

- **Ask for what you want.** Rather than labeling misbehavior as inappropriate or uncooperative, tell students the specific behaviors you would like to see instead. Set boundaries to let kids know the options they have or the conditions under which they can enjoy the choices they have. Likewise, instead of talking about how their behavior makes you feel, focus on how their cooperation will pay off for them: "As soon as you return your library book, you can take another one home," as opposed to "I feel disappointed when you forget to return your book."

- **Take care of yourself.** We are most apt to slip into negative, hurtful behaviors when we haven't had enough sleep or decent nutrition, when we haven't expressed our needs clearly enough, or when we have been so flaky about follow-through that students are tempted to test our limits. Own your behavior and apologize when you blow it. Remember, in a win-win classroom built on mutual respect and cooperation, students can be pretty quick to forgive a lapse, especially when we are willing to take responsibility for it and not try to blame it on something or someone else. Modeling good boundaries and self-care can be one of the most important lessons we teach.

Shifting to the Positive

Probably the most surprising thing about classroom management is that it *isn't* about managing kids at all! It is, instead, about creating an environment of safety and connectedness—along with the necessary instructional and interactive patterns—that builds student *self-management.* The more independent and cooperative your students are, the less time you will need to devote to putting out fires and the more time you will get to actually teach. That, my friends, is the entire point.

Misbehavior can occur for myriad reasons. Power struggles and feelings of humiliation are common causes, but so are out-of-school incidents that we may never know about. Unclear directions and insufficient satisfaction of physical and neurological needs (e.g., for light, auditory stimulation, hydration or nutrition, movement, or using the restroom) can also provoke undesirable behavior. Improper academic placement can also be a problem, whether students are underchallenged and bored, overwhelmed by the amount of work assigned, or unable to perform a task successfully. Many students would rather appear "bad" than "dumb."

As we have seen, many common practices we see in schools—patterns cemented in our own childhood experiences as well as in models we have been taught to use—can create or compound classroom management problems. Fortunately, we have alternatives, and even in extremely toxic school environments, I have seen teachers quietly shut the door and connect with kids in positive, encouraging, and healthy ways. This is the foundation for classroom management success, whether you are just starting out or are a well-established veteran.

We have much to unlearn and many new habits to put in place. These changes will take practice and commitment, so give it time and stick with it. Changing our behavior, like any worthwhile, process-oriented endeavor, requires a long view and a good bit of patience, practice, and support.

Respect the importance of connectedness. Classroom management begins with relationships. Researcher Robert Blum and colleagues (Blum, McNeely, & Rinehart, 2004) note that "people connect with people before they connect with institutions." Their work has shown that connecting with kids in school can lead to a decrease in a wide range of risk factors, including students' disruptive and violent behavior. The researchers emphasize the role of the teacher in creating the kind of emotionally safe climate in which the incidence of negative, antisocial behaviors are less likely to occur.

Most important, always remember what brought you to teaching. (Whatever your reasons, I doubt they included the opportunity to yell at kids.) And know that you are making a difference. With every lesson, every word, every look, and every smile, you have the potential to change a life. So let's choose the tools that will allow us to do so in the most positive, effective ways possible.

To give your feedback on this publication and be entered into a drawing for a free ASCD Arias e-book, click here or type in this web location: **www.ascd.org/ariasfeedback**

ENCORE

MOTIVATION & RESPONSE STRATEGIES AND TOOLS

Ineffective, Destructive Approaches	Effective, Safe Approaches
• Discounting the importance of connectedness	• Building positive relationships and connections with students
• Disregarding the importance of building students' interpersonal skills and sense of community	• Building a sense of community and mutual respect among students; developing social skills; promoting peer tutoring, mentoring
• Creating rules (and more rules)	• Providing sensible boundaries
• Focusing on punishments and negative consequences (even if logical)	• Focusing on positive outcomes or consequences (e.g., earned access to privileges)
• Disregarding nonverbal cues and emotional energy in classroom	• Paying attention to nonverbal cues and emotional energy in classroom
• Using reactive approaches, taking students' behavior personally, labeling and criticizing students, making students wrong	• Using proactive approaches, not taking students' behavior personally, attacking problems rather than people
• Approving students conditionally on the basis of desirable behavior	• Accepting students unconditionally, valuing them as people

Ineffective, Destructive Approaches	Effective, Safe Approaches
• Using praise as management tool (e.g., connecting desirable behavior to teacher approval, labeling student characteristics such as intelligence)	• Using recognition (e.g., connecting desirable behavior to desirable outcome unrelated to teacher approval, acknowledging student actions such as making effort)
• Delivering commands, limiting students' access to options, fearing student autonomy	• Offering students choices, encouraging student autonomy (within limits)
• Providing unclear instructions, making assumptions about students' understanding or processing of information	• Providing clear instructions in ways students can understand
• Failing to provide structure and routines	• Providing structure and routines
• Failing to immediately follow through, delaying follow-through with warnings or by asking for excuses	• Following through immediately, withdrawing or withholding privileges when infractions occur
• Telling students how their behavior makes you feel, labeling misbehavior	• Asking for what you want, telling students what they need to do to be successful or get what they want

continued

Ineffective, Destructive Approaches	Effective, Safe Approaches
• Dismissing, ignoring, criticizing, or interfering with students' emotions; blaming students; trying to "fix" students' feelings or problem situations	• Listening to and validating students' emotional experiences
• Reacting to, criticizing, or punishing emotional outbursts; escalating or compounding emotional energy	• Expressing understanding of and concurrence (agreement) with students' emotional expression; defusing emotional energy
• Giving advice or commands, rescuing or enabling students, telling students how to solve problems	• Building students' problem-solving skills
• Depending on students' fear of your anger or disapproval to motivate good behavior	• Controlling anger, using meaningful, positive outcomes (unrelated to your emotional state) to motivate positive behavior
• Yelling at or humiliating students, using verbal or physical violence	• Showing respect for students' dignity regardless of their behavior
• Setting expectations	• Setting intentions

Ineffective, Destructive Approaches	Effective, Safe Approaches
• Following curriculum without regard for students' academic needs or abilities	• Accommodating students' needs for success, matching instruction to students' cognitive abilities to move through the curriculum successfully, differentiating as necessary
• Presenting material without regard for how students process information	• Meeting students' learning-style needs, teaching the way students learn
• Expecting behavior from students that they do not see in you	• Modeling respectful and responsible behavior
• Relying on other adults to handle or punish student misbehavior	• Handling student misbehavior while keeping other adults (administrators, parents) informed
• Applying rules rigidly; asking for excuses and giving warnings	• Building in flexibility to rules before problems arise
• Withholding academic credit or advancement from students who misbehave	• Keeping students' behavior separate from academic achievement

Source: From *Book of Handouts* (pp. 155–156), by J. Bluestein, 2013, Albuquerque, NM: ISS Publications. © 2013 by Jane Bluestein. Adapted with permission.

You can find an additional Encore section online at www. ascd.org/ASCD/pdf/books/Bluestein2014Arias.pdf.

References

Barnes, M. (2013, February 11). Throw out rules and consequences, and let your classroom manage itself [Blog post]. *SmartBlog on Education.* Available: http://smartblogs.com/education/2013/02/11/throw-out-rules-and-consequences-and-let-your-classroom-manage-itself

Bluestein, J. (1988). *21st century discipline: Teaching students responsibility and self-management.* New York: Instructor Books.

Bluestein, J. (2001). *Creating emotionally safe schools.* Deerfield Beach, FL: Health Communications.

Bluestein, J. (2008). *The win-win classroom: A fresh and positive look at classroom management.* Thousand Oaks, CA: Corwin.

Bluestein, J. (2010). *Becoming a win-win teacher: Survival strategies for the beginning educator.* Thousand Oaks, CA: Corwin.

Bluestein, J. (2013). *Book of handouts.* Albuquerque, NM: ISS Publications.

Bluestein, J., & Katz, E. (2005). *High school's not forever.* Deerfield Beach, FL: Health Communications.

Blum, R. W., McNeely, C., & Rinehart, P. M. (2004). *Improving the odds: The untapped power of schools to improve the health of teens.* Minneapolis, MN: Center for Adolescent Health and Development, University of Minnesota.

Dweck, C. (2013, September 26). *The effect of praise on mindsets* [Video]. Available: www.youtube.com/watch?v=lp5FvxnC0Ew

National Education Association. (1975). *Code of ethics.* Available: http://www.nea.org/home/30442.htm

RSA. (Producer). (2010). *RSA Edge lecture with Sir Ken Robinson: Changing paradigms* [Video]. Available: www.thersa.org/events/video/archive/sir-ken-robinson

Related Resources

At the time of publication, the following ASCD resources were available (ASCD stock numbers appear in parentheses). For up-to-date information about ASCD resources, go to www.ascd.org. You can search the complete archives of Educational Leadership at http://www.ascd.org/el.

Print Products

Classroom Management That Works: Research-Based Strategies for Every Teacher by Robert J. Marzano, Debra J. Pickering, and Jana Marzano (#103027)

Discipline with Dignity, 3rd Edition: New Challenges, New Solutions by Allen Mendler, Richard Curwin, and Brian Mendler (#108036)

The Educator's Guide to Preventing and Solving Discipline Problems by Mark Boynton and Christine Boynton (#105124)

Inspiring the Best in Students by Jonathan Erwin (#110006)

Leading and Managing a Differentiated Classroom by Marcia B. Imbeau and Carol Ann Tomlinson (#108011)

ASCD PD Online© Courses

Classroom Management: Building Effective Relationships, 2nd Ed. (#PD11OC104)

Classroom Management: Understanding Diverse Learning Needs, 2nd Ed. (#PD11OC110)

Differentiated Instruction: Leading and Managing a Differentiated Classroom (#PD11OC137)

For more information: send e-mail to member@ascd.org; call 1-800-933-2723 or 703-578-9600, press 2; send a fax to 703-575-5400; or write to Information Services, ASCD, 1703 N. Beauregard St., Alexandria, VA 22311-1714 USA.

About the Author

Photo by Steven Bercovitch

Jane Bluestein, Ph.D., is a keynote speaker and seminar leader who has worked with educators worldwide. An award-winning author, her books include *The Win-Win Classroom, Becoming a Win-Win Teacher, Creating Emotionally Safe Schools,* and *Mentors, Masters and Mrs. MacGregor: Stories of Teachers Making a Difference.* Formerly a classroom teacher, crisis intervention counselor, and teacher training program coordinator, she is committed to changing schools one heart at a time. Bluestein currently heads Instructional Support Services, Inc., a consulting and resource firm in Albuquerque, New Mexico. For more information, visit Dr. Bluestein's website at http://janebluestein.com, or contact her at jane@janebluestein.com.

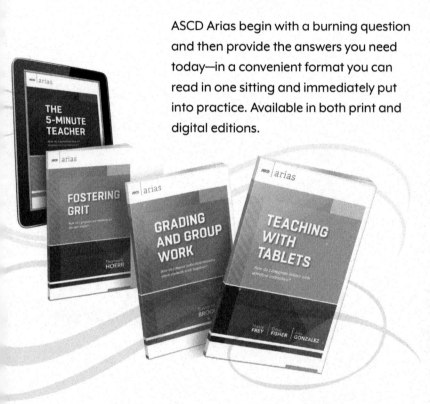

The ASCD Whole Child approach is an effort to transition from a focus on narrowly defined academic achievement to one that promotes the long-term development and success of all children. Through this approach, ASCD supports educators, families, community members, and policymakers as they move from a vision about educating the whole child to sustainable, collaborative actions.

Managing 21st Century Classrooms relates to **all five** tenets.
*For more about the ASCD Whole Child approach, visit **www.ascd.org/wholechild**.*

WHOLE CHILD
TENETS

1 **HEALTHY**
Each student enters school healthy and learns about and practices a healthy lifestyle.

2 **SAFE**
Each student learns in an environment that is physically and emotionally safe for students and adults.

3 **ENGAGED**
Each student is actively engaged in learning and is connected to the school and broader community.

4 **SUPPORTED**
Each student has access to personalized learning and is supported by qualified, caring adults.

5 **CHALLENGED**
Each student is challenged academically and prepared for success in college or further study and for employment and participation in a global environment.

ASCD
LEARN. TEACH. LEAD.